Forces
movement

531

Forces

Karen Bryant-Mole

Heinemann

First published in Great Britain by Heinemann Library, Halley Court, Jordan Hill, Oxford OX2 8EJ
a division of Reed Educational & Professional Publishing Ltd.

OXFORD FLORENCE PRAGUE MADRID ATHENS MELBOURNE AUCKLAND KUALA LUMPUR
SINGAPORE TOKYO IBADAN NAIROBI KAMPALA JOHANNESBURG GABORONE PORTSMOUTH
NH (USA) CHICAGO MEXICO CITY SAO PAULO

Designed by Jean Wheeler
Commissioned photography by Zul Mukhida
Consultant – Hazel Grice
Printed in Hong Kong

00 99 98
10 9 8 7 6 5 4 3 2

British Library Cataloguing in Publication Data

Bryant-Mole, Karen
  Forces. - (Science all around me)
  1. Force and energy - Juvenile literature
  I. Title
  531.1'13

ISBN 0 431 07822 X

A number of questions are posed in this book. They are designed
to consolidate children's understanding by encouraging further
exploration of the science in their everyday lives.

**Words that appear in the text in bold can
be found in the glossary.**

Acknowledgements
The Publishers would like to thank the following for permission to reproduce photographs: Eye Ubiquitous 6, 8; John Heinrich 20;
Tony Stone Images 16; Mike Powell 18; Lori Adamski Peek 22; Andrew Sacks Zefa 4, 10, 12, 14.

Every effort has been made to contact copyright holders of any material reproduced in this book. Any omissions will be
rectified in subsequent printings if notice is given to the Publisher.

Contents

What are forces?

Forces are pushes and pulls.
Forces can make things move.

This bulldozer is acting as a force.
It is pushing the soil into
a big heap.

(i) *Anything that starts moving is being pushed or pulled by something or someone.*

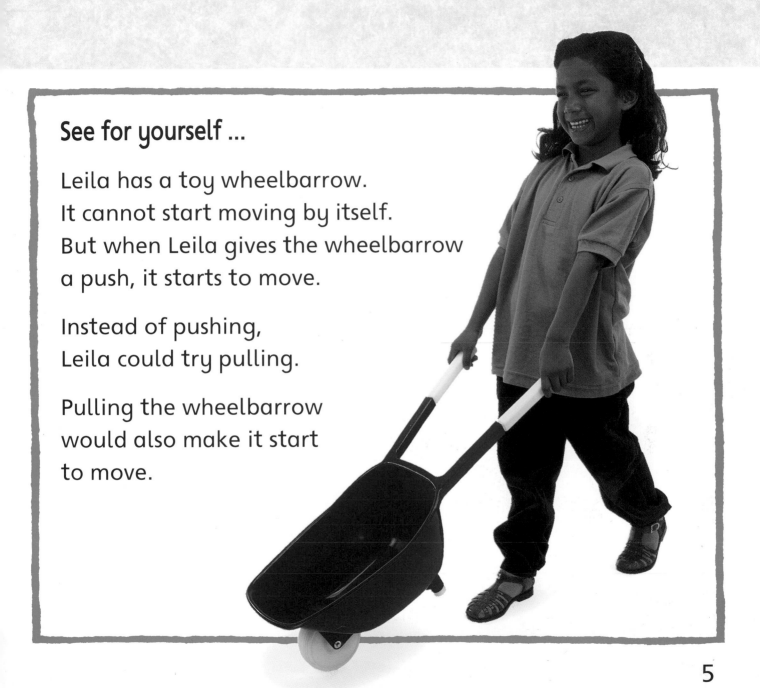

See for yourself ...

Leila has a toy wheelbarrow.
It cannot start moving by itself.
But when Leila gives the wheelbarrow
a push, it starts to move.

Instead of pushing,
Leila could try pulling.

Pulling the wheelbarrow
would also make it start
to move.

5

Forces in nature

Forces are found in the **natural** world all around us.

The wind is pushing this tree and making it bend.

Young plants push soil out of the way, as they come up through the ground.

People are part of nature, too.
We can make pushes and pulls with our bodies.

? *Which part of your body would you use to throw a ball?*

See for yourself ...

Kitty and Yasmin are using their breath to push a ball.

They are blowing through straws and using the push of the air to get the ball to the other end of the box.

The first person to score ten 'goals' is the winner.

Manufactured forces

Pushes and pulls can also be made,
or manufactured, by machines.

The front section of a train is called a locomotive.
This locomotive is powered by an engine which
pushes the locomotive along the track.

The carriages are
moving, too.
They are being pulled
along the track by
the locomotive.

? *Can you think of other vehicles that need engines to make them move?*

See for yourself ...

Tom has a wind-up crab.

As he turns the knob, a strip of metal inside the toy winds up.

When he lets go of the knob, the metal strip starts to unwind. It pushes some small wheels inside the crab which make the crab start moving.

9

Movement

As these racing cars **travel** around the race track, they will slow down, speed up and turn around corners. They have started and they will stop.

Movements like these are all caused by forces. Different types of force produce different types of movement.

? *The cars are moving forwards. What is the opposite of forwards?*

See for yourself ...

Yasmin is playing a game of 'Follow My Leader' with her friends.

Yasmin is the caller. Maya is the leader.

Yasmin can call out, 'start', 'stop', 'faster', 'slower', 'backwards', 'forwards', 'turn left', or 'turn right'.

Everyone has to follow Maya.

Speed

These athletes are lining up to run a race.
The fastest person will be the winner.

People run by pushing against the ground with
their legs and feet.

Runners build up strong **muscles** in their legs
so that they can push hard and run fast.

? *Can you feel your legs and feet pushing when you run?*

See for yourself ...

Jade has given this book a gentle push.
It is sliding slowly across the floor.

When she gives the book a big push,
it slides much more quickly.

The harder the push,
the faster an object will **travel**.

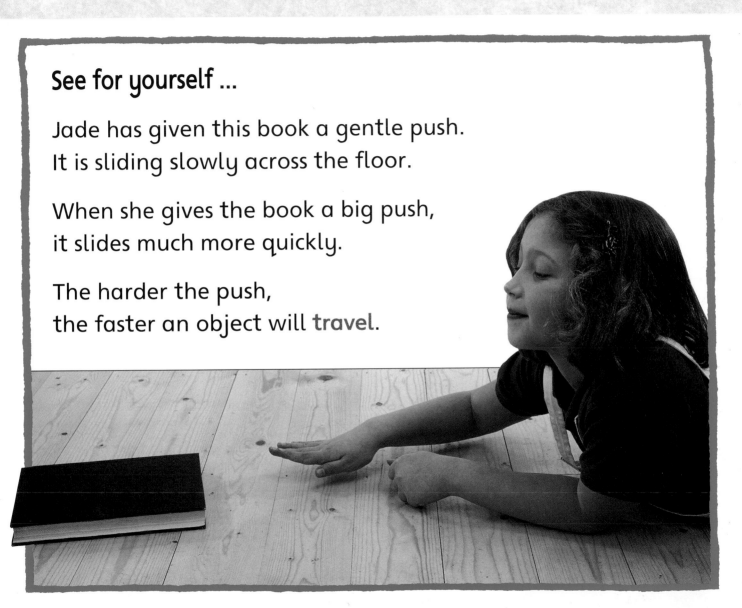

Friction

Friction is a force that slows things down. Friction is caused when two objects rub together.

This golf ball is rubbing against the grass. Tiny, rough pieces on the surface of the ball and the grass push against each other and slow the ball down.

(i) *Friction might stop this ball before it reaches the hole.*

See for yourself ...

Leila has given this toy car a push.
The friction between the car's wheels
and the floor slows the car down.

Eventually, it will stop.

If she tried this on a carpeted floor,
the car would stop more quickly.
Carpet is rougher than smooth wood,
so there is more friction.
The car keeps moving for
less time.

Changing speed

This ice skater can choose how quickly she skates and when to stop.

She **controls** her **speed** by the amount of push she uses.

She uses a lot of push to **travel** quickly but just a little to travel slowly.

To stop, she turns her skates sideways so that more of the skate rubs against the ice.

? *Can you remember what this rubbing is called?*

See for yourself ...

Aliyu is riding his bike. He notices that the harder he pushes on the pedals, the faster he travels.

When he stops pedalling, friction slows the bike down.

Aliyu can control the speed he travels by the amount of push he puts on the pedals.

Brakes

This man is riding his bike along the road.
If he wants to stop, he uses his brakes.
When he squeezes the brakes, rubber pads grip the wheels very tightly.

This creates a lot of friction and stops the bike very quickly.

? *Can you think of anything else that has brakes?*

See for yourself ...

Jade asked her mum to fix a paper plate to a stick, using a drawing pin.

Jade made the plate spin round.

Now she is holding a straw against the edge of the plate.

The friction caused by the plate and the straw rubbing together makes the plate stop spinning.

19

Changing direction

Forces can make things change direction.

Without forces, once this pram was moving it would carry on in a straight line.
So, when the baby's father wants to turn a corner, he has to make forces act on the pram.

He pulls back with one hand and pushes forwards with the other hand.

? What do car drivers use to change direction?

See for yourself ...

Aliyu is pushing a toy shopping trolley. When he pushes it in a straight line, he is pushing with both hands.

But when he pushes it around the chair, he notices that he is pushing with his left hand and pulling with his right hand.

21

Changing shape

Forces can also make things change shape.

The baker in this picture has made bread dough. He stretches and squashes the dough.

Stretches and squashes are types of forces. They are special sorts of pulls and pushes that change the shape of something.

? *Can you think of other things that can be stretched and squashed?*

See for yourself ...

Yasmin has some play dough.
Play dough is squashy.
It is easy to change its shape
in many different ways.

She can squash it
and stretch it.
She can twist it
and bend it
and roll it, too.

Glossary

controls   is in charge of

muscles   bundles of thin bands that move parts of the body

natural   part of nature, not made by people

speed   how fast something goes

travel   go from place to place

vehicles   things that take people or goods from place to place

Index